EASY PIANO

2019 GREATEST
POP & MOVIE HITS

Produced by
Alfred Music
P.O. Box 10003
Van Nuys, CA 91410-0003
alfred.com

Printed in USA.

ISBN-10: 1-4706-4248-4
ISBN-13: 978-1-4706-4248-8

Cover Photos:
Abstract vector background: © iStock Images Plus via Getty Images / Godruma • Colorful blurred lights: © iStock-Getty Images Plus via Getty Images / thanasus •
Colorful explosion: © iStock-Getty Images Plus via Getty Images / Pattadis Walarput

CONTENTS

ALWAYS REMEMBER US THIS WAY

(from *A Star Is Born*)

Words and Music by
Lady Gaga, Natalie Hemby,
Hillary Lindsey and Lori McKenna

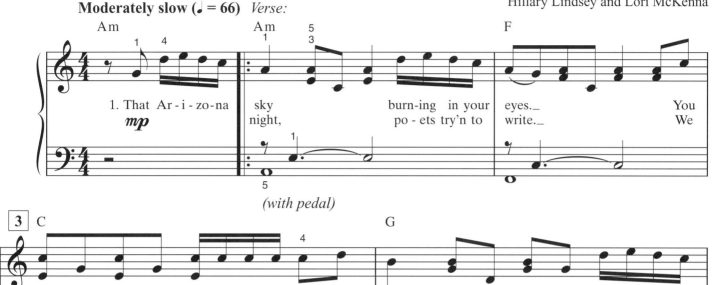

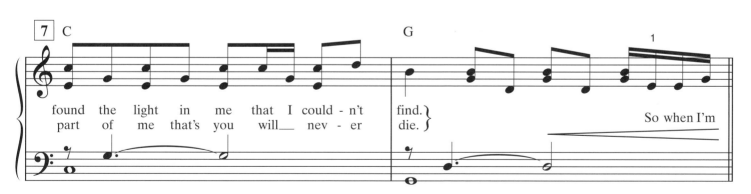

Always Remember Us This Way - 3 - 1

BAD LIAR

Words and Music by
Jorgen Odegard, Benjamin McKee, Daniel Reynolds,
Daniel Platzman, Wayne Sermon and Aja R. Volkman

8

BREATHIN

Words and Music by
Ilya, Ariana Grande,
Savan Kotecha and Max Martin

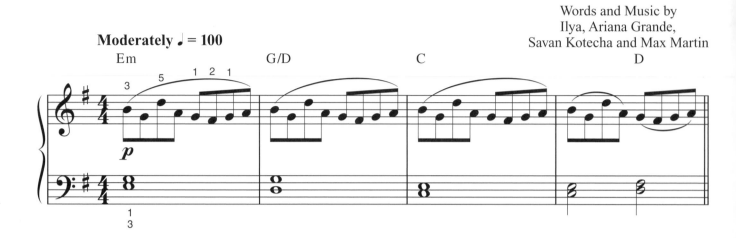

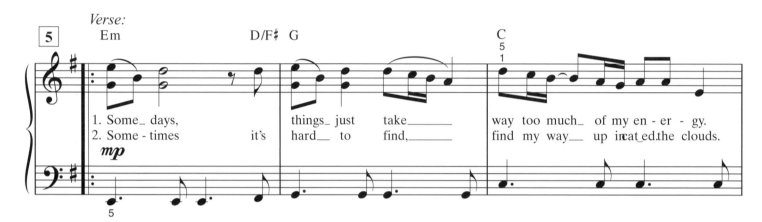

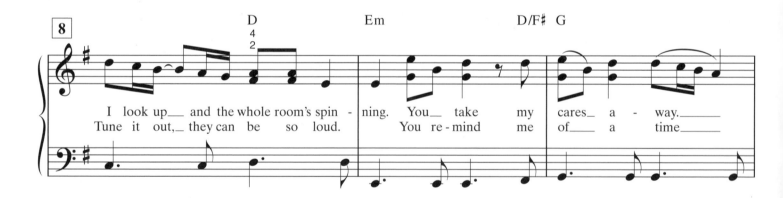

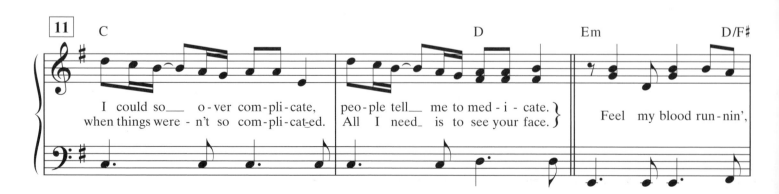

Breathin - 3 - 1

12

FANTASTIC BEASTS THEME

(from *Fantastic Beasts: The Crimes of Grindelwald*)

Composed by
James Newton Howard

Slowly, freely ♩ = 80

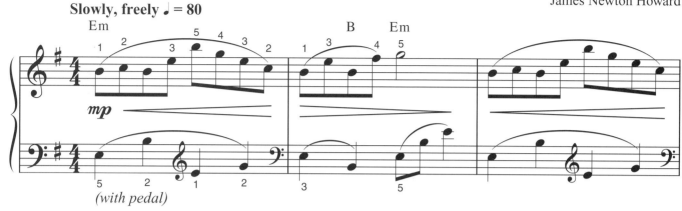

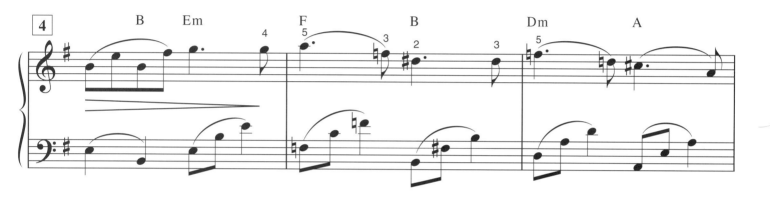

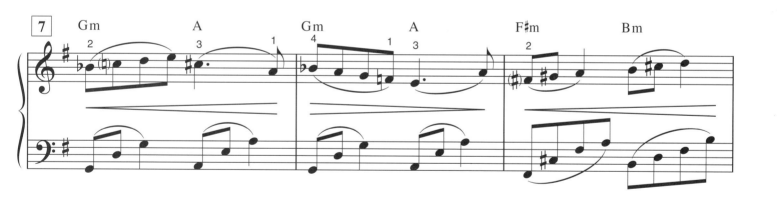

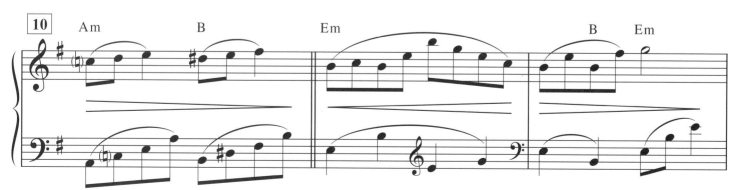

Fantastic Beasts Theme - 3 - 1

14

GIRL LIKE YOU

Words and Music by
Josh Mirenda, Jaron Boyer and Michael Tyler

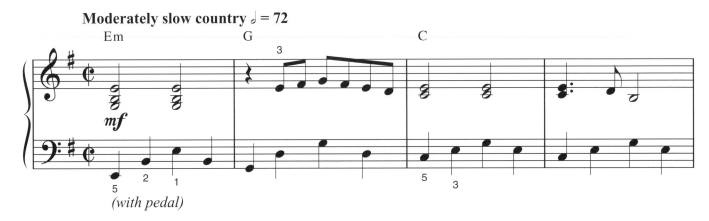

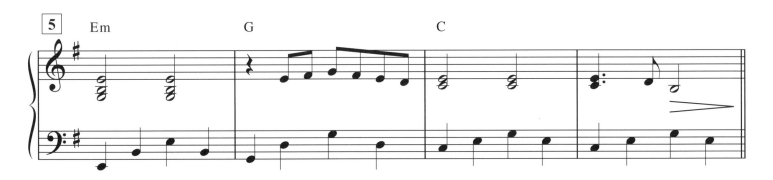

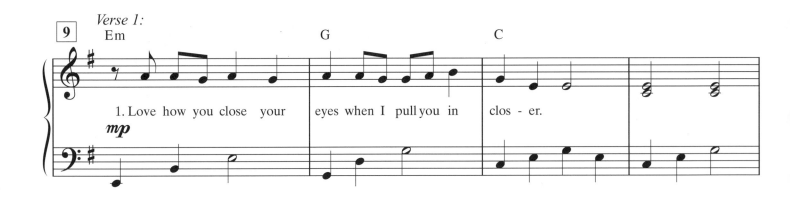

18

Girl Like You - 5 - 3

GIRLS LIKE YOU

Words and Music by Klenord Raphael,
Henry Walter, Belcalis Almanzar, Gian Stone,
Jason Evigan, Brittany Hazzard and Adam Levine

Moderately, with a half-time feel (♩ = 60) (♩ = 120)

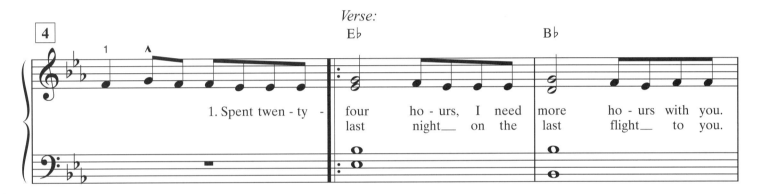

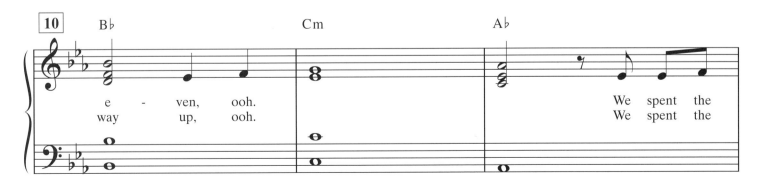

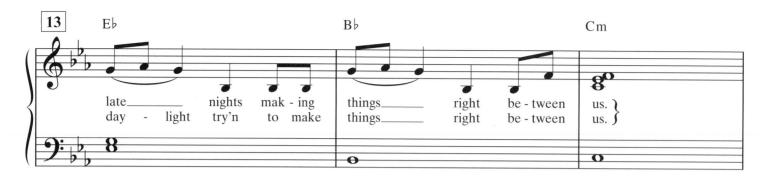

13 Eb / Bb / Cm

late _____ nights mak-ing / things _____ right be-tween us. }
day - light try'n to make / things _____ right be-tween us. }

16 Ab / Eb / Bb

But now it's all good,_ babe. Roll that back - wood,_ babe, and play me

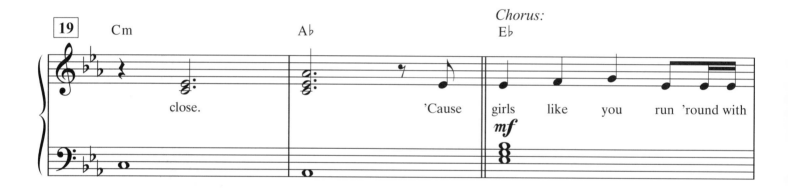

Chorus:

19 Cm / Ab / Eb

close. 'Cause girls like you run 'round with

mf

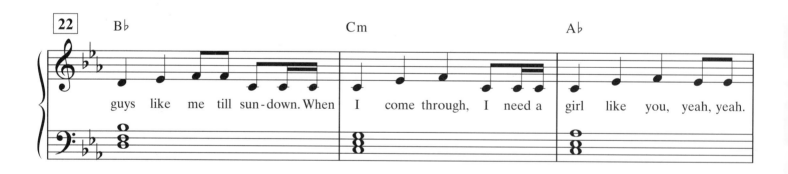

22 Bb / Cm / Ab

guys like me till sun-down. When I come through, I need a girl like you, yeah, yeah.

25 Eb / Bb / Cm

Girls like you love fun, and yeah, me too. What I want when I come through, I need a

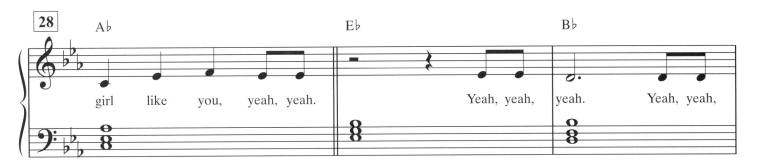

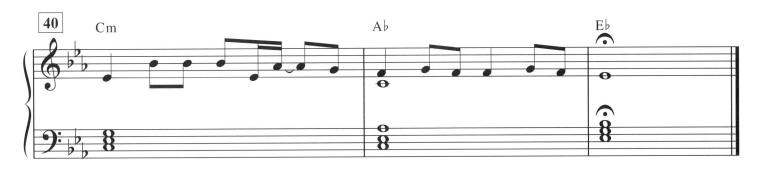

Girls Like You - 3 - 3

HIGH HOPES

Words and Music by
Tayla Parx, Brendon Urie, Ilsey Juber,
Jacob Sinclair, Janny Owen Young, Jonas Jeberg,
Lauren Pritchard, Sam Hollander and William Lobban Bean

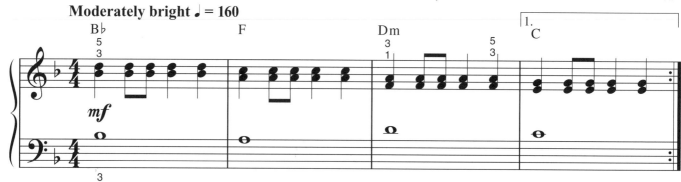

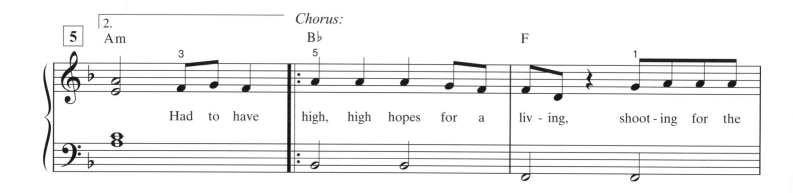

High Hopes - 5 - 1

26

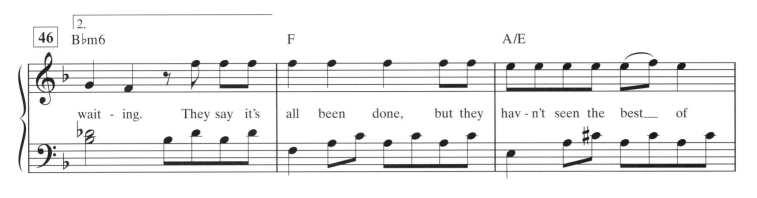

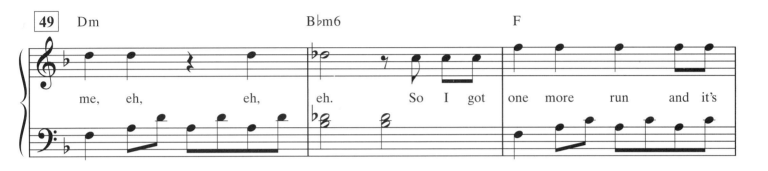

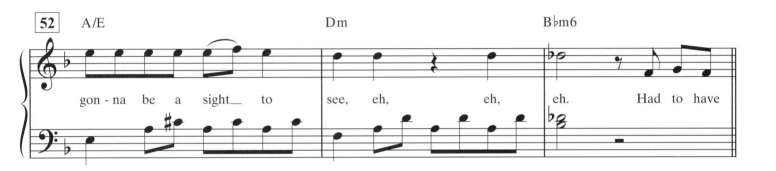

Chorus:

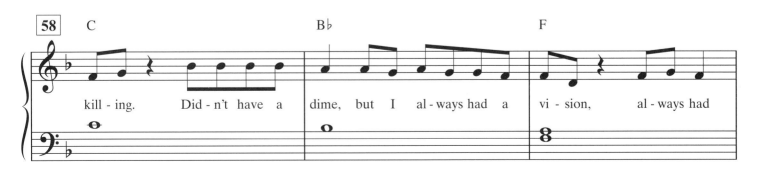

I'LL NEVER LOVE AGAIN

(from *A Star Is Born*)

Words and Music by
Lady Gaga, Natalie Hemby,
Hillary Lindsey and Aaron Raitiere

I'll Never Love Again - 5 - 1

30

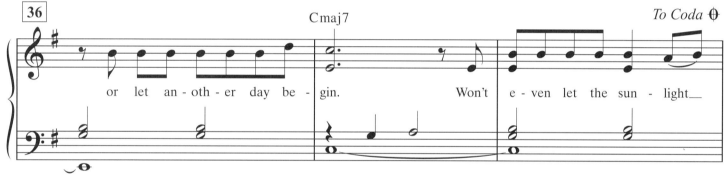

32

IS THAT ALRIGHT?
(from *A Star Is Born*)

Words and Music by
Lady Gaga, Paul Blair,
Nick Monson, Lukas Nelson,
Mark Nilan Jr. and Aaron Raitiere

Moderately, with expression (♩ = 103)

Is That Alright? - 3 - 1

LETA'S THEME

(from *Fantastic Beasts: The Crimes of Grindelwald*)

Composed by
James Newton Howard

Slowly and tenderly ♩. = 67

(with pedal)

Leta's Theme - 3 - 1

Leta's Theme - 3 - 3

LOVE THEME FROM *CRAZY RICH ASIANS*

By Brian Tyler

Slowly and tenderly ♩ = 85

Love Theme from *Crazy Rich Asians* - 3 - 1

Love Theme from Crazy Rich Asians *- 3 - 2*

42

MEANT TO BE

Words and Music by
Josh Miller, Tyler Hubbard,
David Garcia and Bebe Rexha

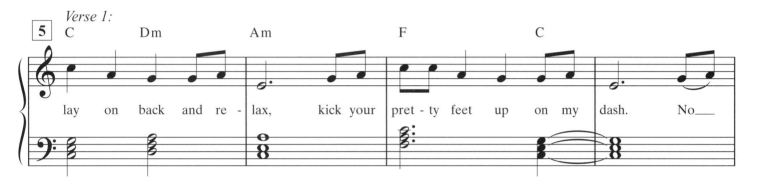

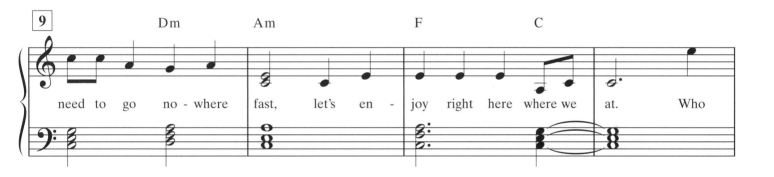

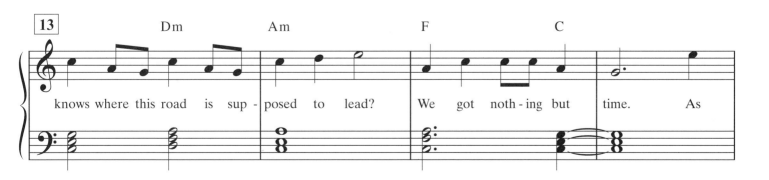

Meant to Be - 5 - 1

44

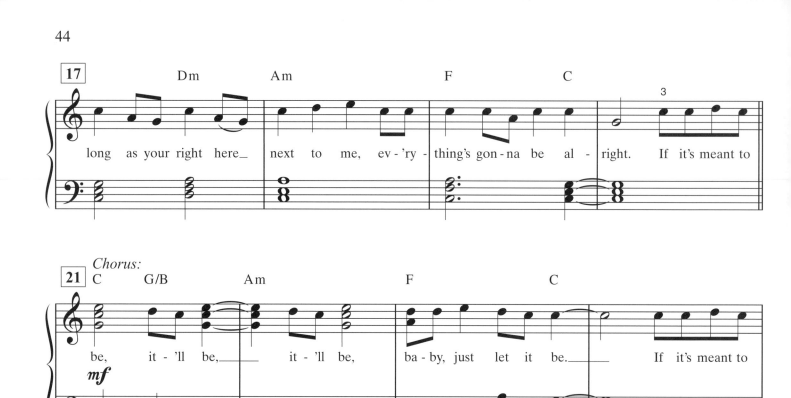

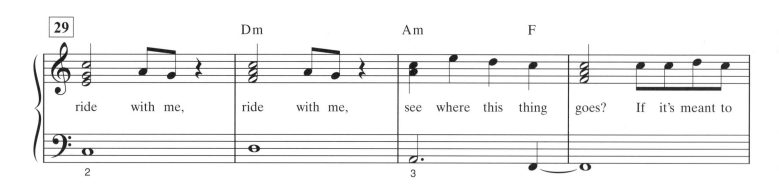

Meant to Be - 5 - 2

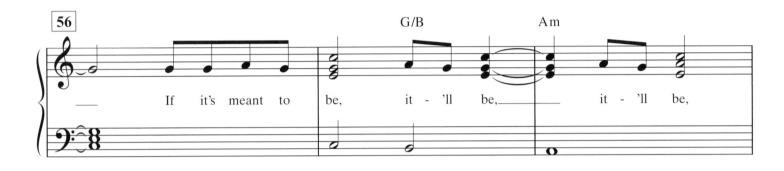

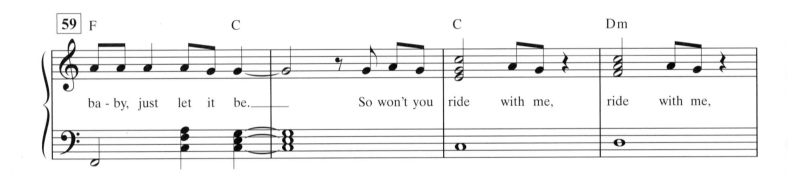

THE PLACE WHERE LOST THINGS GO

(from *Mary Poppins Returns*)

Lyrics by
Scott Wittman and Marc Shaiman

Music by
Marc Shaiman

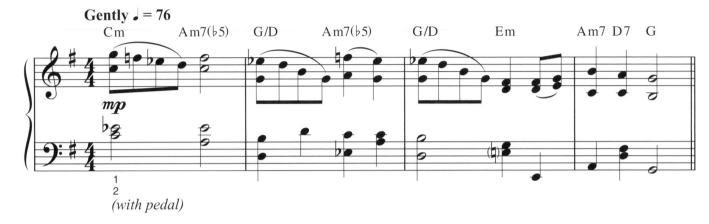

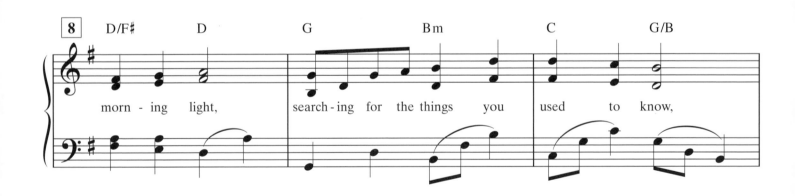

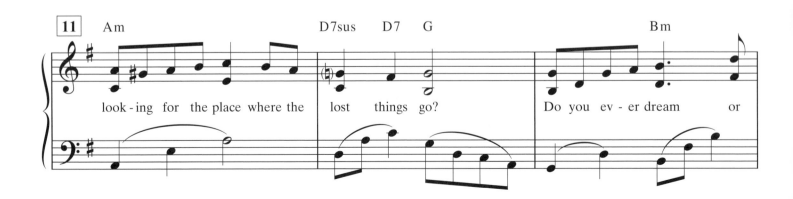

The Place Where Lost Things Go - 3 - 1

50

The Place Where Lost Things Go - 3 - 3

RAINBOW

Words and Music by
Kacey Musgraves, Shane McAnally
and Natalie Hemby

Slowly ♩ = 64

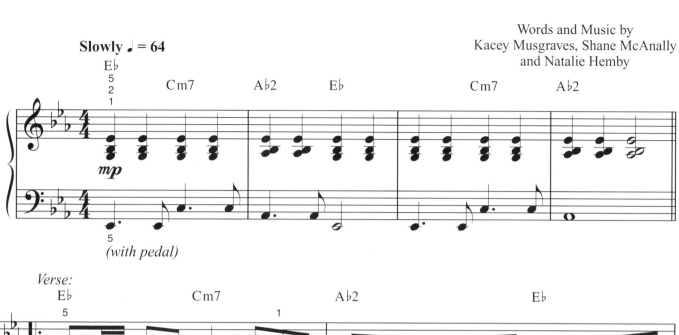

(with pedal)

Verse:

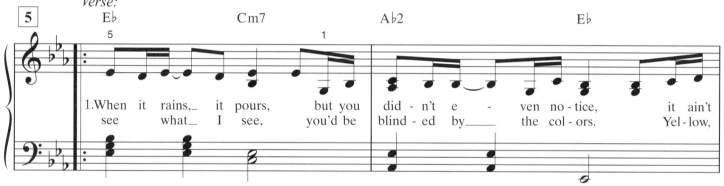

1.When it rains,__ it pours, but you did-n't e - ven no - tice, it ain't
see what__ I see, but you'd be blind-ed by__ the col-ors. Yel-low,

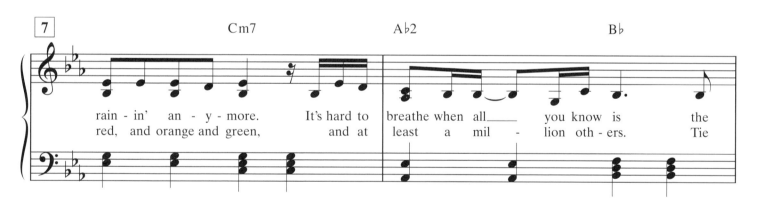

rain - in' an-y-more. It's hard to breathe when all__ you know is the
red, and orange and green, and at least a mil - lion oth-ers. Tie

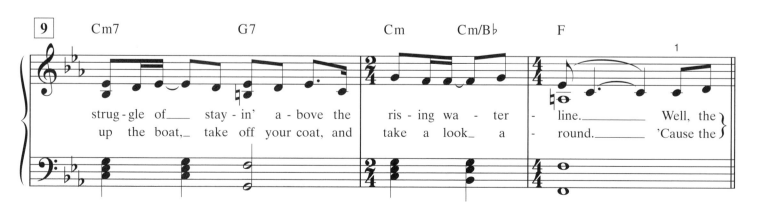

strug-gle of__ stay-in' a-bove the ris-ing wa-ter-line.__ Well, the
up the boat,__ take off your coat, and take a look__ a - round.__ 'Cause the

Rainbow - 3 - 1

52

Rainbow - 3 - 2

SHALLOW

(from *A Star Is Born*)

Words and Music by
Lady Gaga, Mark Ronson,
Anthony Rossomando and Andrew Wyatt
Arranged Tom Gerou

Moderate folk rock ♩ = 96

Shallow - 5 - 1

56

Shallow - 5 - 3

58

Shallow - 5 - 5

SUNFLOWER

Words and Music by
Austin Richard Post, Carter Lang, Louis Bell,
Khalif Brown, Billy Walsh and Carl Rosen

Moderately slow ♩ = 88

Need-less to say I keep her in check. She was all bad, bad nev-er-the-less.

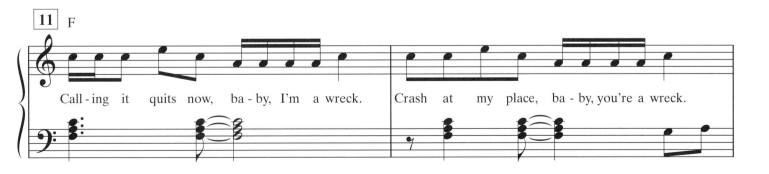

Call-ing it quits now, ba-by, I'm a wreck. Crash at my place, ba-by, you're a wreck.

Sunflower - 5 - 1

62

TEQUILA

Words and Music by
Dan Smyers, Jordan Reynolds and Nicolle Galyon

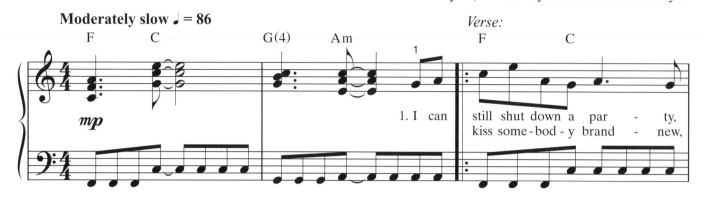

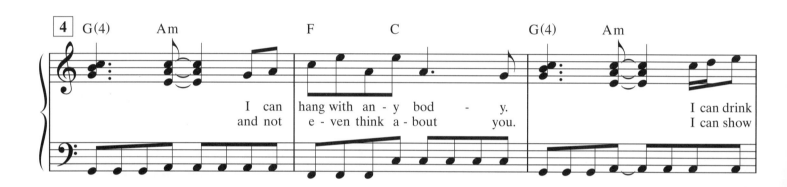

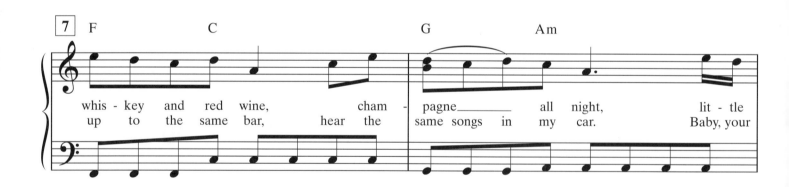

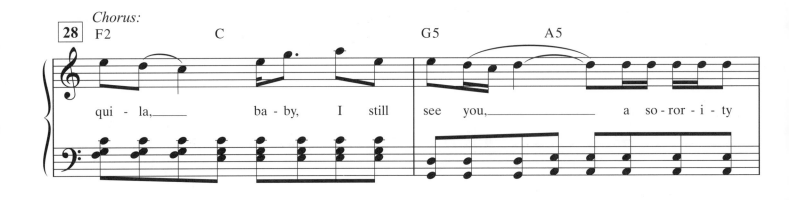

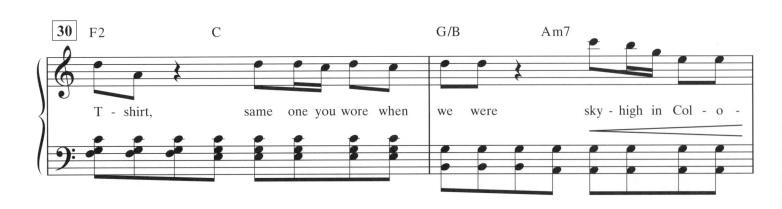

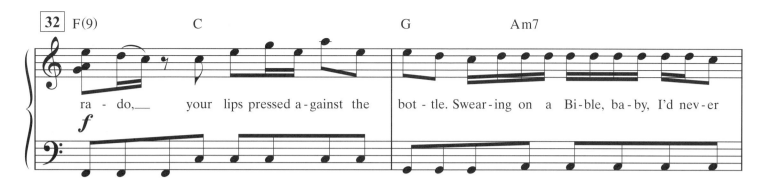

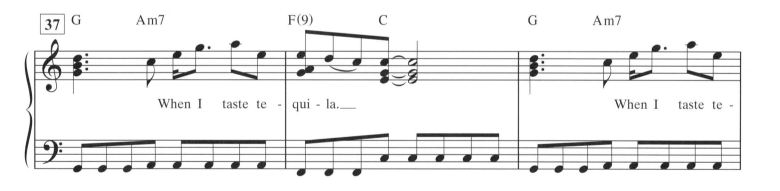

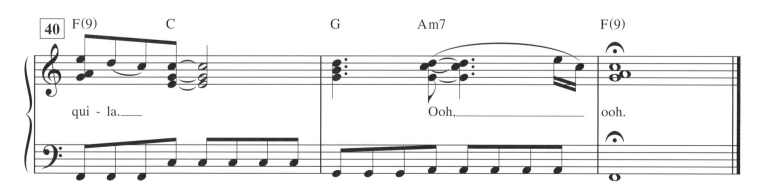

YOU SAY

Words and Music by
Paul Mabury, Lauren Ashley Daigle
and Jason Ingram

Slowly ♩ = 72

(with pedal)

Verse 1:

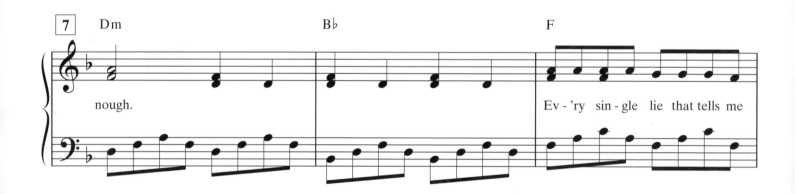

1.I keep fight-ing voic-es in my mind that say I'm not e-

nough. Ev-'ry sin-gle lie that tells me

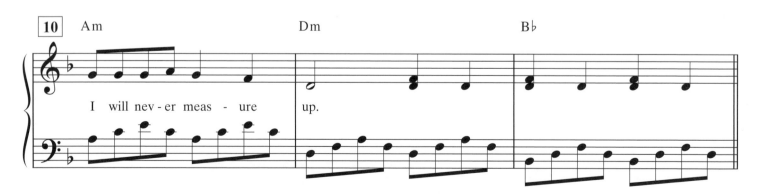

I will nev-er meas-ure up.

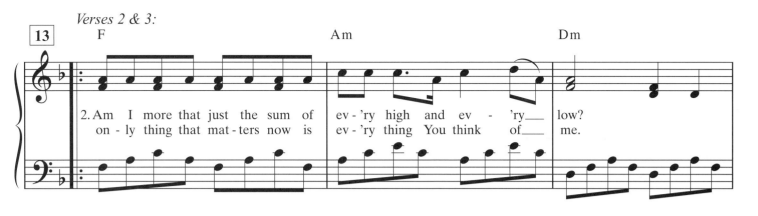

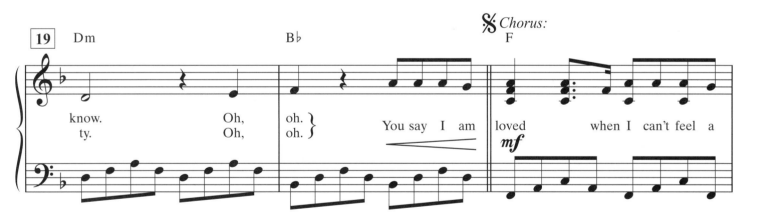

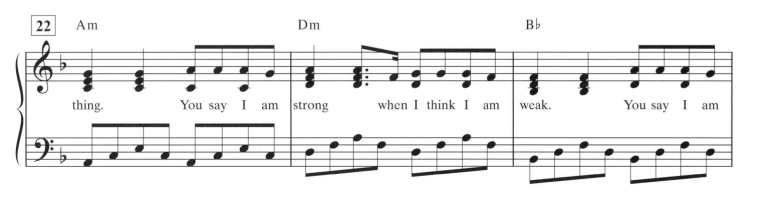

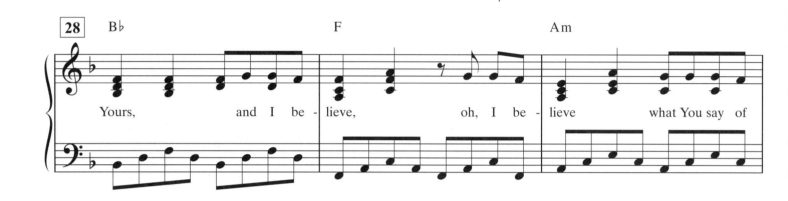

Bridge:

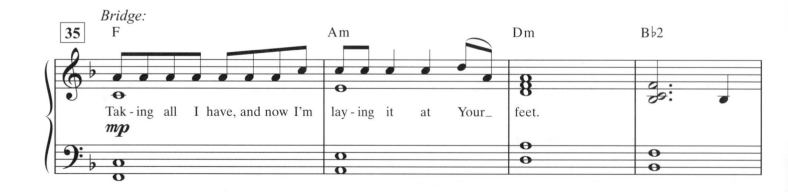

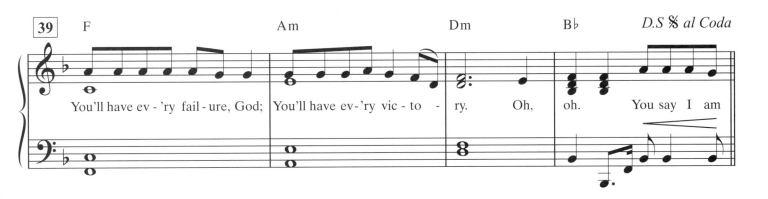

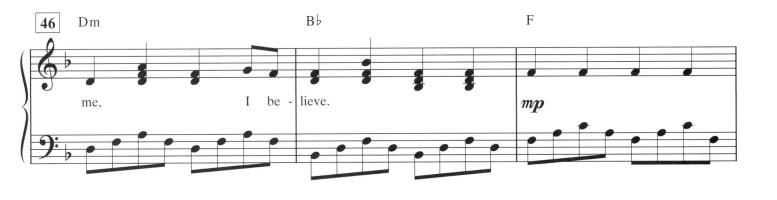

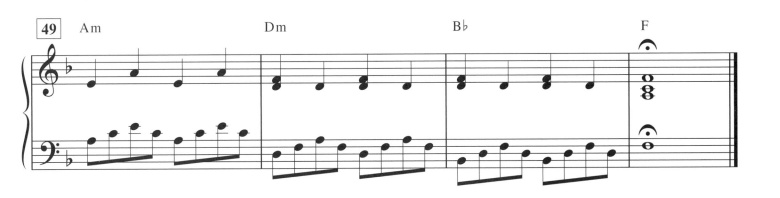

WONDERFUL LIFE

(from *Smallfoot*)

Words and Music by
Wayne Kirkpatrick and Karey Kirkpatrick

(with pedal)

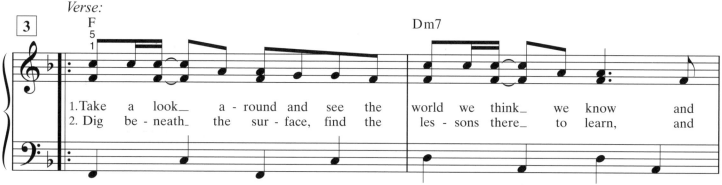

Verse:

1. Take a look_ a - round and see the world we think_ we know and
2. Dig be - neath_ the sur - face, find the les - sons there_ to learn, and

then look clos - er. There's more to life_ than meets the eye, a
then dig deep - er. Feed your in - tu - i - tion; don't leave

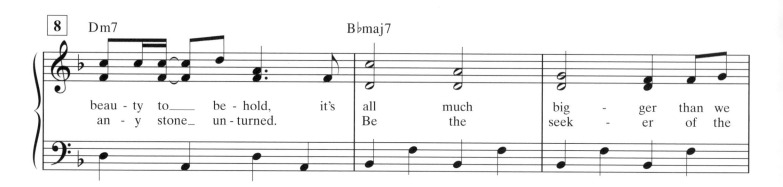

beau - ty to__ be - hold, it's all much big - ger than we
an - y stone_ un - turned. Be the much the seek - er of the

73

Wonderful Life - 3 - 2

74

Wonderful Life - 3 - 3